Ultimate ROMANTIC SHOWSTOPPERS

Project Managers: Carol Cuellar and Zobeida Pérez
Art Design: Ken Rehm
Text By: Fucini Productions, Inc.
Special thanks to David, Larry, Gail, Vincent, Mike, and Ken for their creative input

MW00826616

CONTENTS

Ultimate ROMANTIC SHOWSTOPPERS

Introduction

Cupid, the timeless symbol of love, is invariably depicted carrying a bow and arrow. More appropriate would be to show him with a bow and *violin*. Or perhaps instead of floating among the clouds, he should be sitting at a piano, because if our classic cherub really wants to penetrate our hearts and stir our amorous desires, he wouldn't turn to arrows, but to song.

Music is the universal language of love. Its power over our passions is unrivaled. It kindles our deepest longings and makes our most romantic moments even softer and sweeter. Like stars in the night sky high over the sea, music guides new lovers through the deep and mysterious passions that await them. Has there ever been a pair of lovers who have not shared their own songs? Like a language known only to the two of them, these songs convey a world of thoughts, feelings, hopes, and dreams that they alone share.

The hearts of lovers beat to the rhythm of love songs. Through this special kind of music, we dream expectantly about the promise of love, celebrate its rich fulfillment, and cherish its special memories.

Romance and music are linked as surely as two lovers.

Trying to imagine love without music is akin to thinking of a feast without food. Indeed, it was Shakespeare who described music as "the food of love." So enjoy this lover's banquet of romantic songs. Our feast includes many courses, from the innocent "Don't Know Much" to the spicier "Me and Mrs. Jones" to the soaring "The Last Time I Felt Like This."

Love songs speak to the romantic in everyone; single ballads have often been recorded by artists of many different musical stripes. The great Erroll Garner's "Misty" is a beautiful example of such a song. A self-taught prodigy who began playing piano professionally at the age of ten, Garner wrote "Misty" as a jazz composition. Later, the lyrics were added by Johnny Burke.

Garner's understated but elegant music combined with Burke's open, almost plaintive lyrics made "Misty" one of the world's most popular love songs. What head-over-heels lover could fail to identify with lines like, "Look at me, I'm as helpless as a kitten up a tree"? And who cannot be moved by the romantic devotion expressed in, "Walk my way, and a thousand violins begin to play"?

Fittingly, "Misty" was recorded by a wide range of great artists in addition to Garner himself. This diverse group includes Duke Ellington, Dakota Staton, Sarah Vaughan, Johnny Mathis, Lloyd Price, the Vibrations, Richard "Groove" Holmes, Kenny Rogers, Eddie "Lockjaw" Davis, and Ray Stevens.

When the American Society of Composers, Authors and Publishers (ASCAP) selected the 25 Most Performed Songs of the 20th Century in December 1999, "Misty" was duly included on this list.

"Misty" was also central to the hit Clint Eastwood movie *Play Misty for Me*. A feast for music lovers, this 1971 film introduced mainstream audiences to another—and until then overlooked—romantic masterpiece, Roberta Flack's moving "The First Time Ever I Saw Your Face."

Written by Scottish folk musician and dramatist Ewan MacColl, this soulful love song had been recorded by Flack earlier but hadn't received wide airplay. Exposure in the hit movie catapulted the song to No. 1 on the *Billboard* chart, a position it held for six weeks. Another Flack love song that reached the top spot was the breezy and sophisticated 1974 tune "Feel Like Makin' Love."

Like "Misty," two other great love songs from an earlier era, "As Time Goes By" and "I Only Have Eyes for You," also made ASCAP's prestigious Top 25 list.

Written by Herman Hupfeld, a Broadway singer, dancer, and composer, "As Time Goes By" may well be the most famous movie love song of all time. It was the theme song for *Casablanca,* the classic Humphrey Bogart–Ingrid Bergman romantic film set against a backdrop of World War II in North Africa. Hupfeld's hauntingly beautiful song is a tribute to the enduring power of love.

The world changes, life has its ups and downs—indeed "time goes by"—and we can do nothing to stop it. Yet, as Hupfeld reminds us, "It's still the same old story" and "the fundamental things apply," so "a kiss is still a kiss," "a sigh is just a sigh," and "the world will always welcome lovers." Who could argue with the wisdom conveyed in these lyrics?

Hupfeld's song, with its affirmation of love's permanence and power, was reassuring to audiences that saw *Casablanca* in the dark and frightening days of 1942. Moviegoers also responded to Dooley Wilson's rendition of the song in the film. A gifted vocalist and drummer, Wilson played the role of Sam, the piano player at the cafe owned by Humphrey Bogart's "Rick" character. (Although Wilson sings "As Time Goes By" in the movie, the actual piano playing is done by Warner Bros. studio musician Elliott Carpenter.) Composer Max Steiner worked "As Time Goes By" so well into his soundtrack for *Casablanca* that the love story and the love song became almost inseparable.

Following the success of *Casablanca,* Hupfeld's song became a major hit and one of the most frequently requested piano lounge tunes. Fans of the composer even erected a plaque at the Robin Hood Inn in Clifton, New Jersey, where Hupfeld wrote "As Time Goes By" in 1931, 11 years before the movie was made.

Hupfeld originally wrote "As Time Goes By" for *Everybody's Welcome*, a Broadway musical revue. The song enjoyed modest success as a show tune and was even recorded by popular band-leader Rudy Vallee. A young dramatist named Murray Burnett was so taken with "As Time Goes By" that he worked the song into *Everybody Comes to Rick's*, a play he was writing. This script eventually served as the springboard for *Casablanca*, and Hupfeld's song was cast in the role that would make it one of the most famous love tunes of all time.

The classic love song "I Only Have Eyes for You" was also featured in a hit movie, the 1934 film *Dames*. Written by the prolific composer Harry Warren, with lyrics by Al Dubin, the subtle but smoldering passion running through this song has mesmerized generations of lovers and music fans.

"I Only Have Eyes for You" was one of many great hits penned by Warren. Born in Brooklyn, New York, as Salvatore Guaragna (he changed his name while working as a musician), Warren wrote more than 300 songs in his long career, including such classics as "Lullaby of Broadway," "Chattanooga Choo Choo," "You Must Have Been a Beautiful Baby," "Shuffle Off to Buffalo," and "That's Amore." He invariably shunned the limelight, so the millions of people who hummed his tunes never knew his name.

Warren's music for films earned him three Academy Awards. "I Only Have Eyes for You" was not among his Oscar winners, but the sensuality of this beautiful song has with-stood the test of time, and it is still one of our most popular love songs. Hit recordings of the song have been made by artists as diverse as the doo-wop group The Flamingos, Art Garfunkel, and Frank Sinatra.

The inimitable Sinatra used his smooth, relaxed style to create many love-song classics. His 1966 recording of "Strangers in the Night" introduced a new generation of fans to the legendary Sinatra sound. Written by composer Bert Kaempfert, with lyrics by Charles Singleton and Eddie Snyder, the song propelled Sinatra back to the top of the pop music scene, providing him with his first No. 1 hit in 11 years. It also earned the singer two Grammy Awards.

"Strangers in the Night" was one of Sinatra's last collaborations with the great arranger Nelson Riddle. Years earlier, the two worked together on another renowned love song, Cole Porter's "I've Got You Under My Skin." Universally regarded as one of America's greatest composers, the Harvard-educated Porter brought a sense of sophistication and urbanity to his songs that made them easy to enjoy on many different levels.

Porter's music was not only a pleasure to listen to, but it was also rewarding for artists

to perform. In addition to Sinatra, artists who recorded "I've Got You Under My Skin" include Ella Fitzgerald, Dinah Washington, Stan Getz, Jackie Gleason, Peggy Lee, Charlie Parker, Gloria Gaynor, Dionne Warwick, Tony Bennett, Bill Evans, Oscar Peterson, Julio Iglesias, and the Four Seasons.

In contrast to the laid-back style of romantic tunes like "I've Got You Under My Skin," other love songs move us through the sheer power of their deeply felt emotions. This was clearly the case with one of the most unforgettable love songs of all time, "When a Man Loves a Woman."

First released by Percy Sledge in 1966, the song embodied the deep soul sound that combined African-American blues with a gritty Southern country sound. Sledge's genuine and stirring rendition of this love song gave it a sense of passion and urgency that touched music fans everywhere. His version of the song reached the top of both the pop and R&B charts.

Like many great love songs, "When a Man Loves a Woman" lived on well past its initial release. In 1987, the song was featured in a commercial for blue jeans in the U.K. Riding this attention, it was released again and reached No. 2 on the British charts.

Michael Bolton covered "When a Man Loves a Woman" on his 1991 album, *Time, Love & Tenderness*. The song became the centerpiece of the No. 1 album, which sold more than six million copies. Bolton's rendition of the song also topped the charts as a single and earned him a Grammy Award for Best Male Pop Vocal Performance.

In 1994, Sledge and the original version of the song gained a new generation of fans when his recording of it was featured on the soundtrack to the Meg Ryan–Andy Garcia film *When a Man Loves a Woman*. The enduring success of this classic offers added proof that great love songs, like true love, only get better with age.

Romantic Song Trivia

• "Smoke Gets in Your Eyes" was originally intended to be an up-tempo tap-dancing tune, until Jerome Kern and Otto Harbach reworked it into a melancholy love song. It debuted in the 1933 musical *Roberta*. More than a quarter of a century later, the doo-wop group The Platters had a No. I hit with the song.

• Maureen McGovern was working as a secretary in 1973 when she was hired to sing the theme song for *The Poseidon Adventure*. This gig led to her singing a string of romantic movie theme hits, including "Can You Read My Mind?" from *Superman*.

• Francine Hurd and Herb Feemster became one of the most popular romantic pop and R&B duos in the 1960s as Peaches and Herb. After recording a string of romantic hits, the duo returned to their native Washington, D.C., and retired to private life. Francine (Peaches) became a homemaker, and Herb joined the police department. By the late 1970s, Herb wanted to return to recording. He teamed up with a new singer, Linda Greene, called her Peaches, and in 1979 released one of the most popular love songs of all time, the No. I hit "Reunited."

• Many love songs come from movies, but few are from cartoon flicks. Linda Ronstadt and James Ingram's 1986 hit "Somewhere Out There" is somewhat unusual since it was the theme of an animated feature, *An American Tail*.

MISTY

Lyric by
JOHNNY BURKE

Music by
ERROLL GARNER

Misty - 3 - 1

AS TIME GOES BY

Words and Music by
HERMAN HUPFELD

As Time Goes By - 2 - 1

I ONLY HAVE EYES FOR YOU

Words by
AL DUBIN

Music by
HARRY WARREN

Are the Stars out to-night?__ I don't know if it's cloud-y or bright__ 'Cause I

on-ly have eyes ____ for you, _____ dear. ____ The moon may be

high, __ but I can't see a thing in the sky, __ 'Cause I on-ly have eyes ____ for

you _____ I don't know if we're in a gar - den, __

I Only Have Eyes for You - 2 - 1

SOMEWHERE OUT THERE

Words and Music by
JAMES HORNER, BARRY MANN
and CYNTHIA WEIL

Somewhere Out There - 5 - 1

LOVE WON'T LET ME WAIT

Words and Music by
VINNIE BARRETT and BOBBY ELI

Love Won't Let Me Wait - 3 - 1

BACK AT ONE

Words and Music by
BRIAN McKNIGHT

CAN YOU READ MY MIND?

(Love Theme from "Superman")

Words by
LESLIE BRICUSSE

Music by
JOHN WILLIAMS

Can you read my mind? Do you know what it is you do to me?___ Don't know who you are. Just a friend from an-oth-er star. Here I am ___ like a kid out of school, hold-ing

Can You Read My Mind? - 3 - 1

AIN'T NO WOMAN
(Like The One I've Got)

Words and Music by
DENNIS LAMBERT and BRIAN POTTER

Ain't No Wo-man like the one I love.___ She can build me

BETCHA BY GOLLY WOW

Words and Music by
THOM BELL and LINDA CREED

Betcha By Golly Wow - 4 - 1

BREATHE

Words and Music by
STEPHANIE BENTLEY
and HOLLY LAMAR

Slowly ♩ = 60

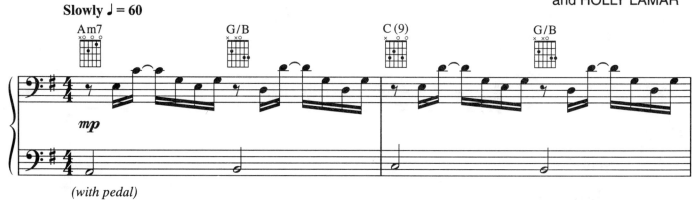

(with pedal)

Verse 1:

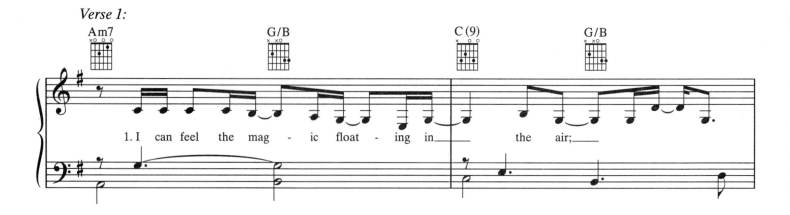

1. I can feel the mag - ic float - ing in____ the air;____

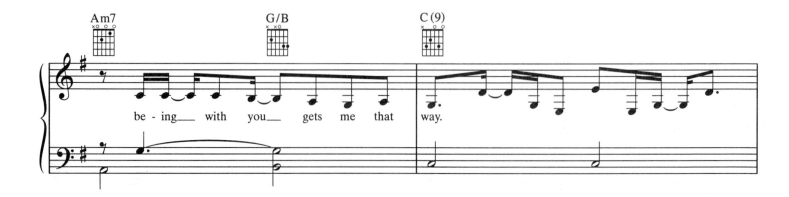

be - ing____ with you____ gets me that way.

Breathe - 5 - 1

that the way___ that love's___ sup-posed___ to be? I can feel you

dim. *mp*

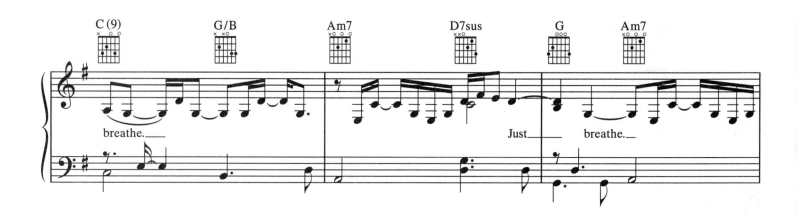

breathe.___ Just___ breathe.___

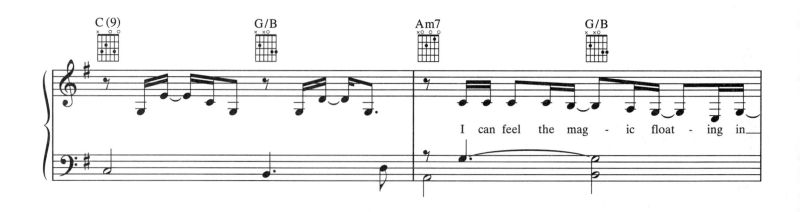

I can feel the mag - ic float - ing in___

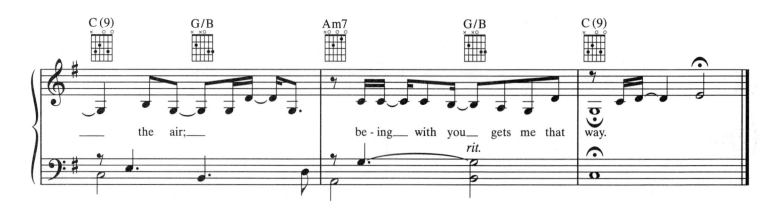

___ the air;___ be-ing___ with you___ gets me that way.

rit.

EUROPA
(Earth's Cry Heaven's Smile)

Music by
CARLOS SANTANA
and TOM COSTER

BY THE TIME THIS NIGHT IS OVER

Words and Music by
MICHAEL BOLTON, ANDY GOLDMARK
and DIANE WARREN

By the Time This Night Is Over - 6 - 1

YOU ARE EVERYTHING

Words and Music by
THOM BELL and LINDA CREED

THE COLOUR OF LOVE

Words and Music by
WAYNE BRATHWAITE, BARRY J. EASTMOND,
BILLY OCEAN and JOLYON SKINNER

The Colour of Love - 7 - 1

COULD IT BE I'M FALLING IN LOVE

Words and Music by
MELVIN STEALS and MERVIN STEALS

Moderate

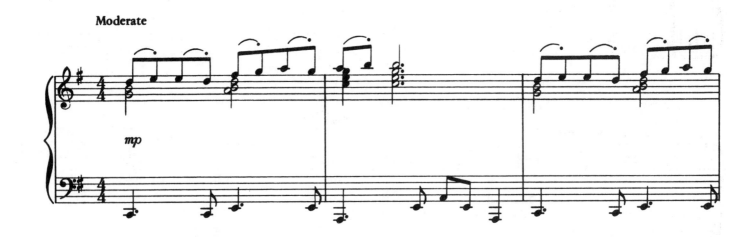

Could It Be I'm Falling in Love - 4 - 1

DON'T KNOW MUCH

(aka All I Need To Know)

Lyric by
CYNTHIA WEIL

Music by
TOM SNOW and BARRY MANN

Tenderly

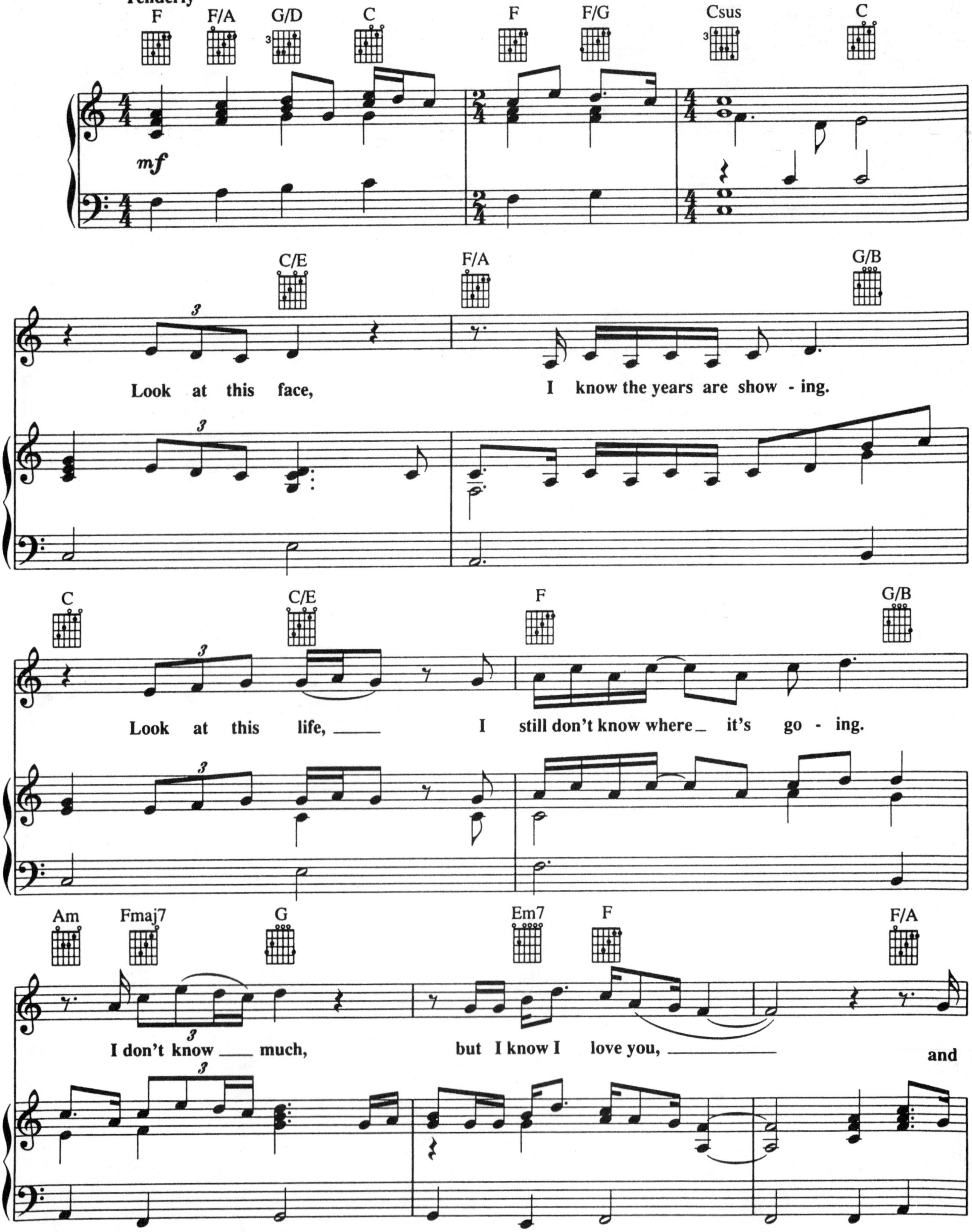

F F/A G/D C F F/G Csus C
mf
C/E F/A G/B
Look at this face, I know the years are show - ing.
C C/E F G/B
Look at this life, I still don't know where it's go - ing.
Am Fmaj7 G Em7 F F/A
I don't know much, but I know I love you, and

DREAMING OF YOU

Words and Music by
TOM SNOW and
FRANNE GOLDE

Moderately ♩ = 88

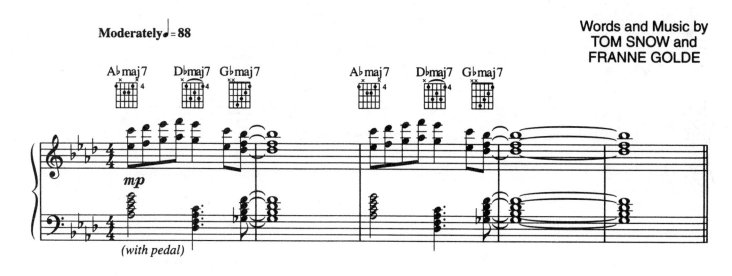

(with pedal)

Verse:

1. Late at night when all the world___ is sleep-ing, I stay up and think of you.___ And I

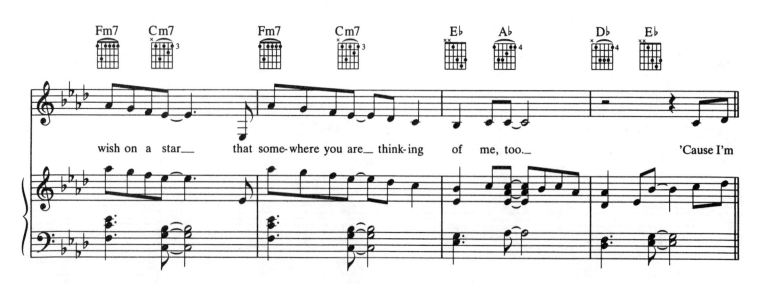

wish on a star___ that some-where you are___ think-ing of me, too.___ 'Cause I'm

Dreaming of You - 6 - 1

Chorus:

dream-ing___ of you to-night.___ Till to-mor-row,___ I'll be

hold-ing you tight.___ And there's no-where in___ the world I'd rath-er be than

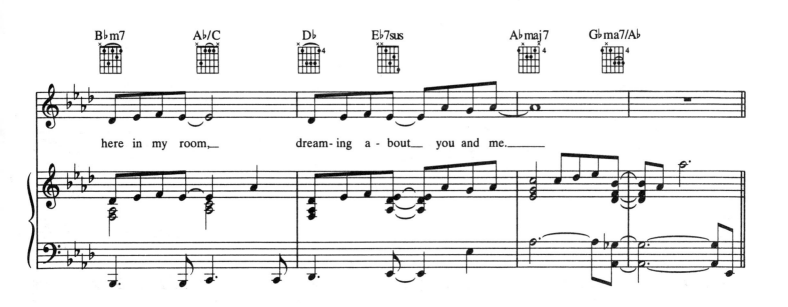

here in my room,___ dream-ing a-bout___ you and me.___

CAN'T STOP MY HEART
From Loving You   (The Rain Song)

Words and Music by
DIANE WARREN

THE FIRST TIME EVER
I SAW YOUR FACE

Words and Music by
EWAN MacCOLL

The First Time Ever I Saw Your Face - 2 - 1

2. The first time ever I kissed your mouth,
   I felt the earth move in my hand,
   Like the trembling heart of a captive bird
   That was there at my command, my love
   That was there at my command.

3. The first time ever I lay with you
   And felt your heart beat close to mine,
   I thought our joy would fill the earth
   And last till the end of time, my love,
   And last till the end of time.

HELLO

Words and Music by
LIONEL RICHIE

Chorus:

CAN'T FIGHT THE MOONLIGHT
(Theme from Coyote Ugly)

Words and Music by
DIANE WARREN

Verse:

Can't Fight the Moonlight - 5 - 1

CAN'T STAY AWAY FROM YOU

Words and Music by
GLORIA ESTEFAN

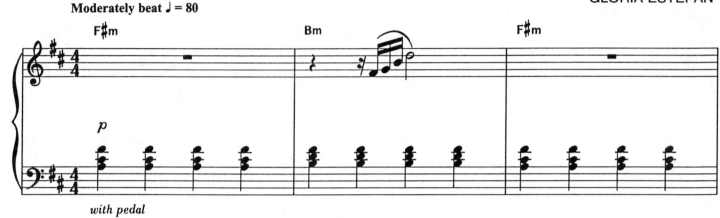

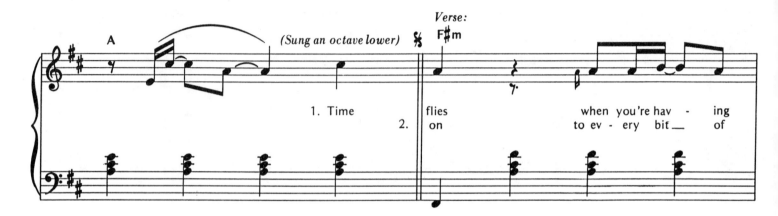

Can't Stay Away From You - 4 - 1

COULD I HAVE THIS KISS FOREVER

Words and Music by
DIANE WARREN

Moderately slow ♩ = 82

1. O - ver____ and o - ver,____ I look in____ your eyes. You are
2. O - ver____ and o - ver,____ I've dreamed of____ this night. Now you're

FEEL LIKE MAKIN' LOVE

Words and Music by
EUGENE McDANIELS

Feel Like Makin' Love - 2 - 1

Feel Like Makin' Love - 2 - 2

FOR ALL WE KNOW

Words by
ROBB WILSON and JAMES GRIFFIN

Music by
FRED KARLIN

Moderato — with a light beat

Love, _____ look at the two of us, _____ Stran - gers _____ in man - y ways. _____ We've got a

For All We Know - 3 - 1

FOR YOUR EYES ONLY

Lyrics by
MICHAEL LEESON

Music by
BILL CONTI

For Your Eyes Only - 3 - 1

HERE WE ARE

Words and Music by
GLORIA ESTEFAN

Slowly ♩ = 66

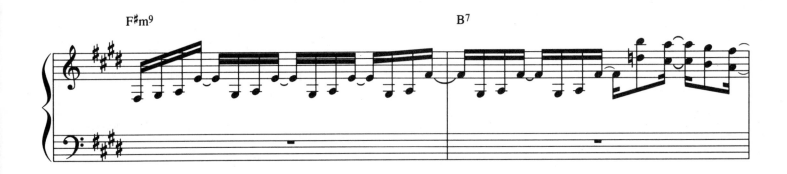

1. Here ___ we

Here We Are - 6 - 1

Bridge:

Here We Are - 6 - 4

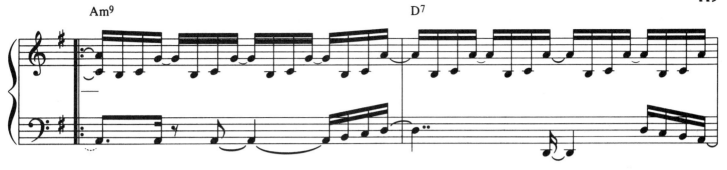

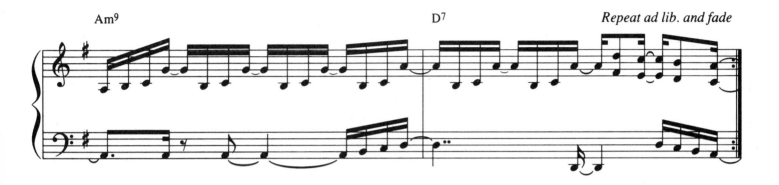

Verse 2:

Here we are all alone;
Trembling hearts, beating strong;
Reaching out, a breathless kiss
I never thought could feel like this.
I want to stop the time from passing by.
I want to close my eyes and feel
Your lips are touching mine.
Baby, when you're close to me,
I want you more each time.
And there's nothing I can do
To keep from loving you.

(To Bridge:)

HOLD ME (IN YOUR ARMS)

Words and Music by
MICHAEL MASSER and LINDA CREED

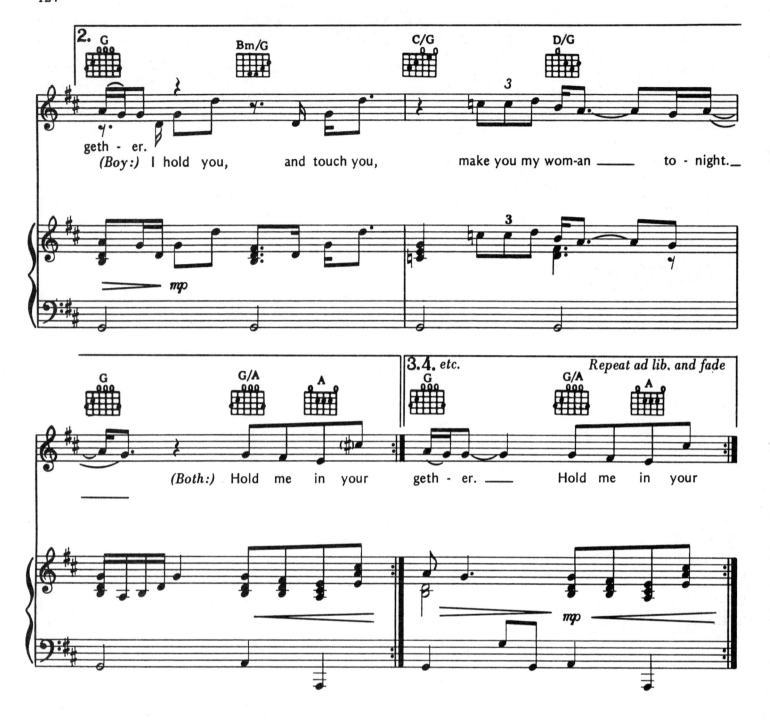

Verse 2:

(Girl:) I believe you, when you say that you love me;
Know that I won't take you for granted.
Tonight the magic has begun.
So won't you hold me, touch me,
Make me your woman tonight?

(Boy:) There's something in your eyes I see
I won't betray your trust in me.

I DO (CHERISH YOU)

Words and Music by
KEITH STEGALL and DAN HILL

*Enharmonic chord labeling of F♭maj7.

I Do (Cherish You) - 5 - 1

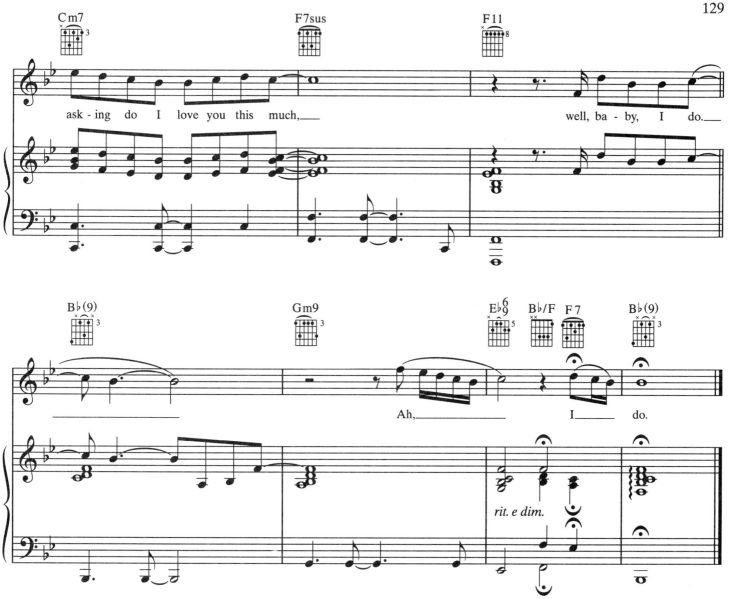

Verse 2:
In my world before you,
I lived outside my emotions.
Didn't know where I was going
Till that day I found you.
How you opened my life
To a new paradise.
In a world torn by change,
Still with all of my heart,
Till my dying day...
(To Chorus:)

HOLD ON TO THE NIGHTS

Words and Music by
RICHARD MARX

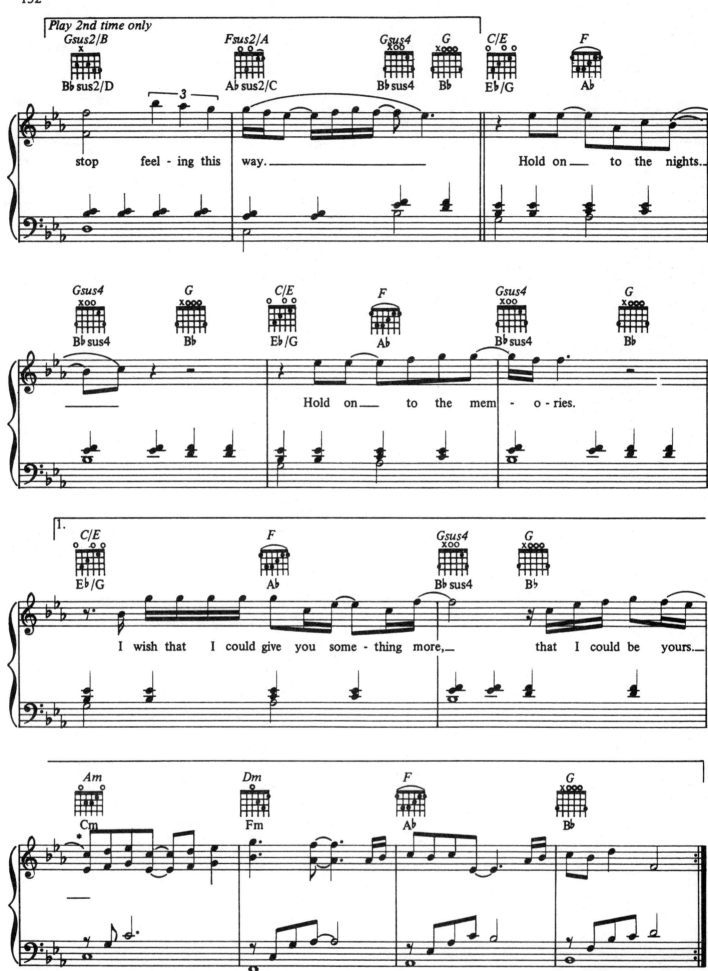

*Vocalists: Hold C for 4 beats.

some-one I've been search-ing for___ is right there.___

Hold on ___ to the nights.___

Hold on ___ to the mem - o - ries.___

cresc.

I wish that I could give   you more.

Oh.

Hold on ___ to the nights. ___

From the Touchstone Motion Picture "CON AIR"

HOW DO I LIVE

Words and Music by
DIANE WARREN

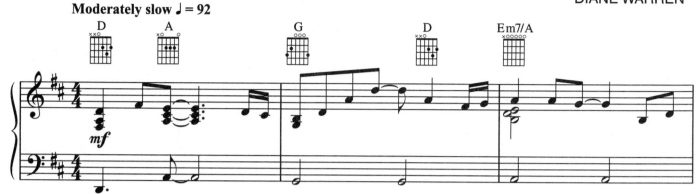

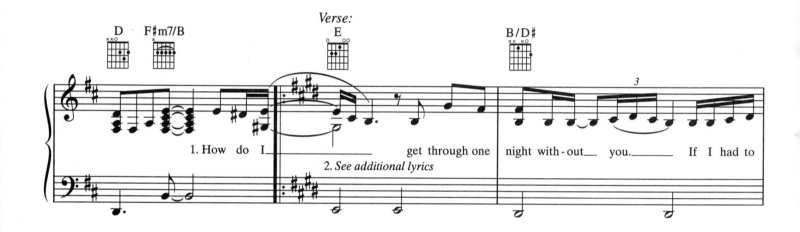

How Do I Live - 4 - 1

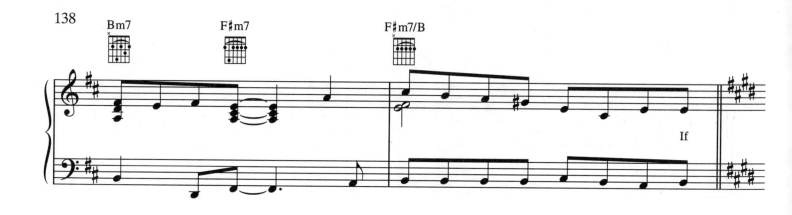

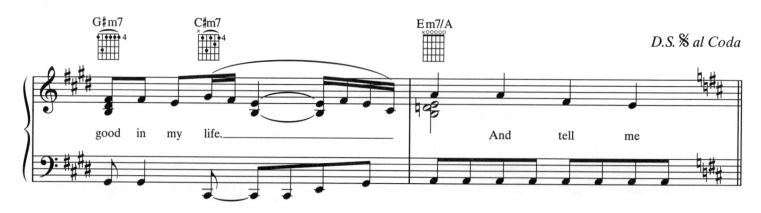

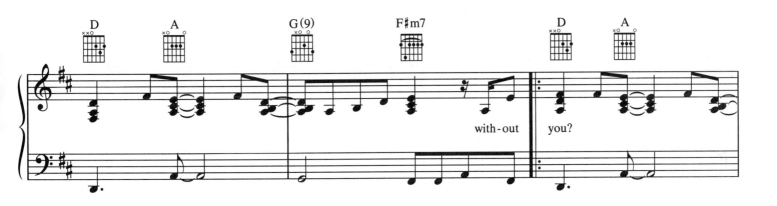

*Repeat ad lib. and fade
(vocal 1st time only)*

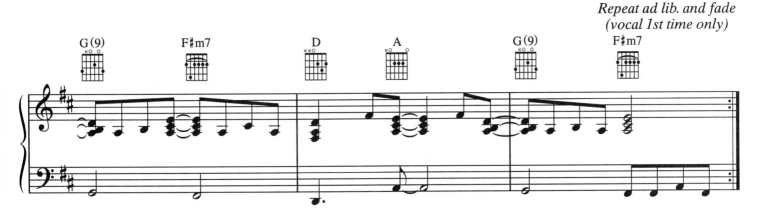

Verse 2:
Without you, there'd be no sun in my sky,
There would be no love in my life,
There'd be no world left for me.
And I, baby, I don't know what I would do,
I'd be lost if I lost you.
If you ever leave,
Baby, you would take away everything real in my life.
And tell me now…
(To Chorus:)

I CAN LOVE YOU LIKE THAT

Words and Music by
STEVE DIAMOND, MARIBETH DERRY
and JENNIFER KIMBALL

From Touchstone Pictures' ARMAGEDDON

I DON'T WANT TO MISS A THING

Words and Music by
DIANE WARREN

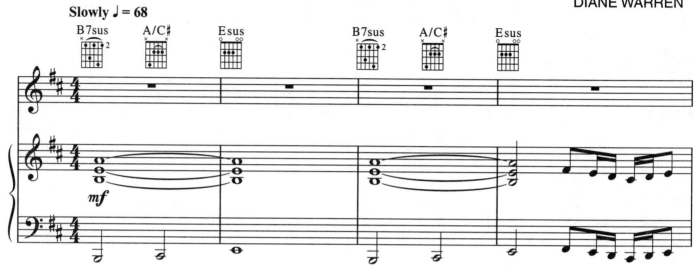

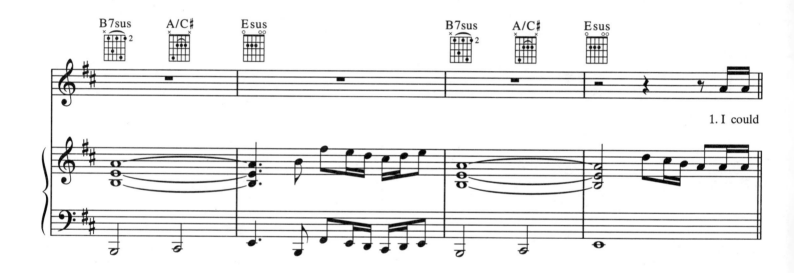

1. I could

Verse 1:

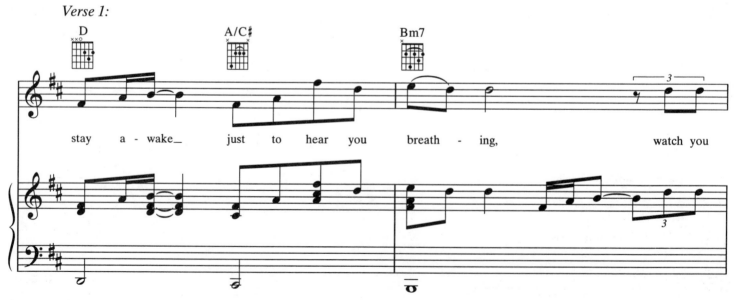

stay a - wake__ just to hear you breath - ing, watch you

I Don't Want to Miss a Thing - 7 - 1

148

Chorus:

I WANT YOU TO NEED ME

Words and Music by
DIANE WARREN

I Want You to Need Me - 5 - 1

I TURN TO YOU

Words and Music by
DIANE WARREN

Chorus:

I WILL ALWAYS LOVE YOU

Words and Music by
DOLLY PARTON

I Will Always Love You - 5 - 1

Verse 3: Instrumental solo

Verse 4:
I hope life treats you kind
And I hope you have all you've dreamed of.
And I wish to you, joy and happiness.
But above all this, I wish you love.
(To Chorus:)

I'VE GOT YOU UNDER MY SKIN

Words and Music by
COLE PORTER

I'VE GOT LOVE ON MY MIND

Words and Music by
CHUCK JACKSON and MARVIN YANCY

I've Got Love on My Mind - 4 - 1

IF EVER YOU'RE IN MY ARMS AGAIN

Lyric by
CYNTHIA WEIL

Music by
TOM SNOW and MICHAEL MASSER

If Ever You're in My Arms Again - 6 - 1

If Ever You're in My Arms Again - 6 - 4

JUST BECAUSE

Words and Music by
MICHAEL O'HARA, ALEX BROWN
and SAM McKINNEY

Just Because - 7 - 1

When I

think a-bout ___ how much I'm lov - ing you, no lim - i -
dia - mond in ___ my mind, a trea - sure found, a pre - cious

ta - tions, no set of reg - i - men - ted rules, ___ I'm a -
gem to me, ___ you're so nice to have ___ a - round. ___ I'm so

mazed how much this love has touched ___ my life, ___ and the com -
glad I took the path that led ___ to this. ___ And it's a -

JUST TO HEAR YOU SAY THAT YOU LOVE ME

Words and Music by
DIANE WARREN

Just to Hear You Say That You Love Me - 5 - 1

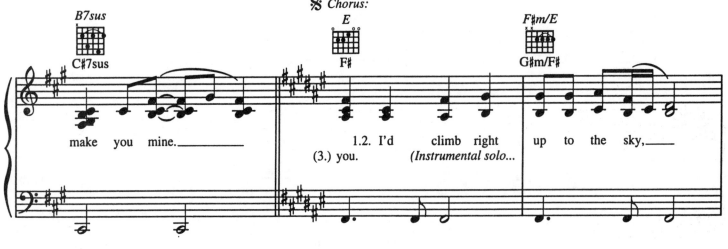

192

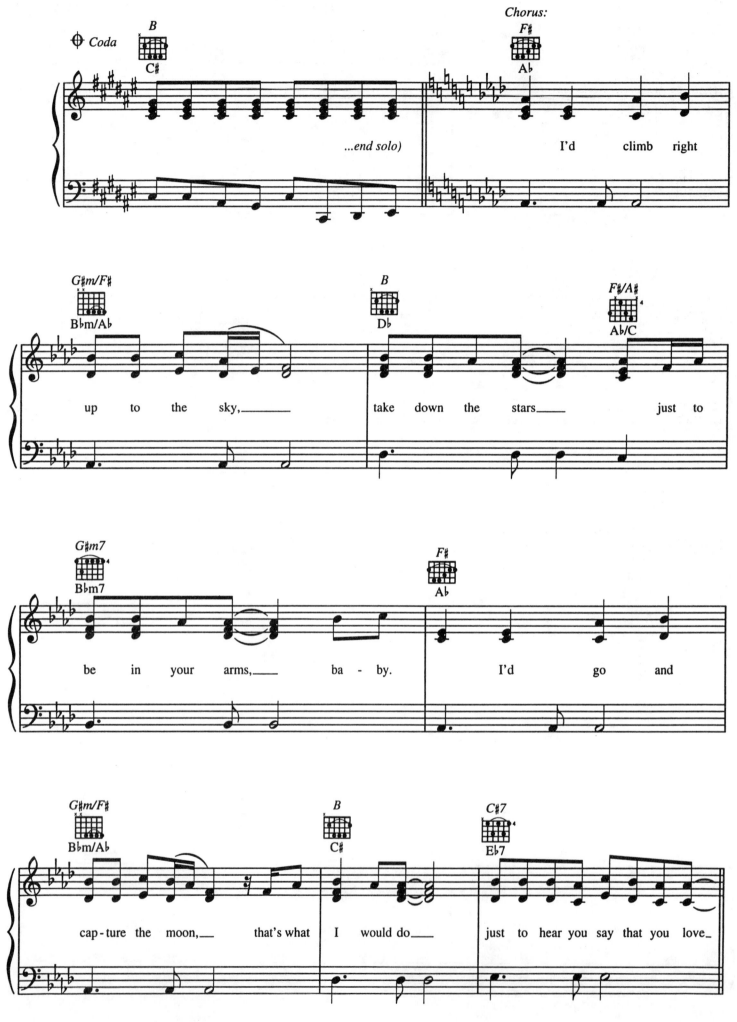

Just to Hear You Say That You Love Me - 5 - 4

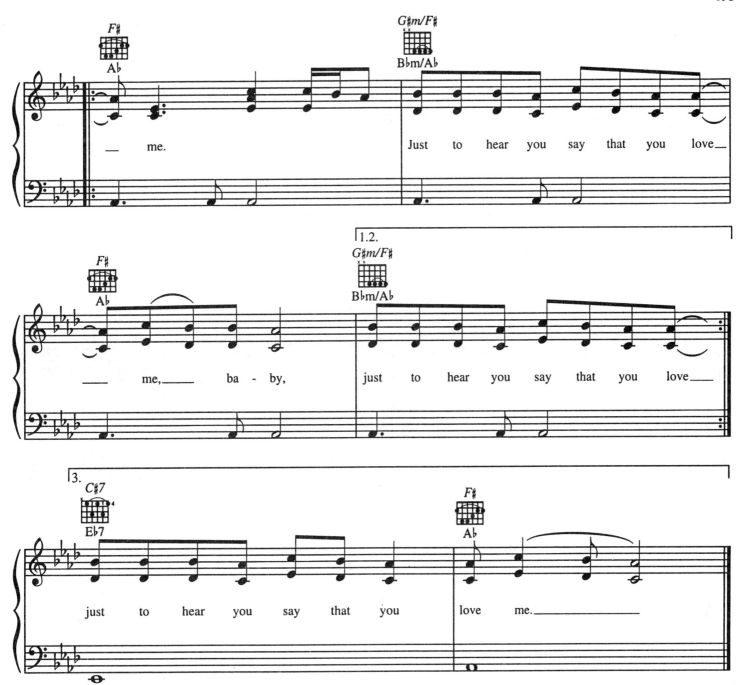

Verse 2:
If I could taste your kiss,
There'd be no sweeter gift heaven could offer, baby.
I want to be the one
Living to give you love.
I'd walk across this world just to be
Close to you, 'cos I want you close to me.
(To Chorus:)

THE LAST TIME I FELT LIKE THIS

Words by
ALAN BERGMAN and MARILYN BERGMAN

Music by
MARVIN HAMLISCH

ME & MRS. JONES

Words and Music by
KENNETH GAMBLE, LEON HUFF
and CARY GILBERT

Me & Mrs. Jones - 5 - 1

LET'S DO IT
(Let's Fall in Love)

Words and Music by
COLE PORTER

Let's Do It - 4 - 1

LET'S MAKE A NIGHT TO REMEMBER

Words and Music by
BRYAN ADAMS and
ROBERT JOHN "MUTT" LANGE

1. I love the way ya look to-night,_ with your hair hang-in' down on your shoul-ders._

'N' I love the way ya dance your slow, sweet tan-go, the way ya wan-na do ev-

Let's Make a Night to Remember - 8 - 1

LOVE IS A WONDERFUL THING

Words and Music by
MICHAEL BOLTON and ANDY GOLDMARK

Moderate Rhythm and Blues

Love Is a Wonderful Thing - 8 - 1

Love Is a Wonderful Thing - 8 - 2

MOONDANCE

Words and Music by
VAN MORRISON

Moondance - 4 - 1

NOBODY DOES IT BETTER

Lyrics by
CAROLE BAYER SAGER

Music by
MARVIN HAMLISCH

OPEN ARMS

Words and Music by
STEVE PERRY and JONATHAN CAIN

Open Arms - 3 - 1

Bridge:

sailed on___ to- geth- er; we drift- ed__ a - part; and here you

are by my__ side.___ So, now I

Chorus:

come_____ to you_____ with o - pen arms;___
here_____ I am_____ with o - pen arms;___

noth - ing_____ to hide, be - lieve what I say._____ So,
hop - ing_____ you see what your

Verse 3:
Living without you; living alone,
This empty house seems so cold.

Verse 4:
Wanting to hold you, wanting you near;
How much I wanted you home.

Bridge:
But now that you've come back;
Turned night into day;
I need you to stay.
(Chorus)

THE ONE

Words and Music by
MAX MARTIN and BRIAN T. LITTRELL

The One - 6 - 1

234

PIANO IN THE DARK

Words and Music by
BRENDA RUSSELL, JEFF HULL
and SCOTT CUTLER

When I find my-self watch-in' the time,___

Piano in the Dark - 5 - 1

si - lence is bro - ken and no words are spo - ken. But oh,___

the dark.

REUNITED

Words and Music by
DINO FEKARIS and FREDDIE PERREN

(Optional 8va bassa throughout)

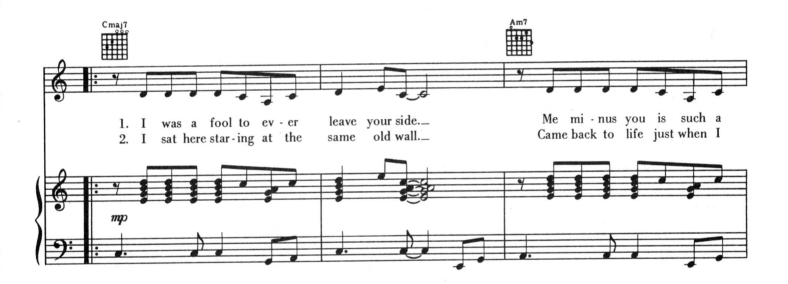

1. I was a fool to ev - er leave your side.__ Me mi - nus you is such a
2. I sat here star - ing at the same old wall.__ Came back to life just when I

lone - ly ride.__ The break-up we had__ has made me lone-some and sad;__ I
got your call.__ I wished I could climb__ right through the tel - e - phone line__ and

Reunited - 3 - 1

3rd Verse:

Lover, lover this is solid love,
  and you're exactly what I'm dreaming of.
All through the day and all through the night,
I'll give you all the love I have with all my might,
  hey, hey!

Lyric for Fade Ending:

Ooo, listen baby, I won't ever make you cry, I won't let one day go by
  without holding you, without kissing you, without loving you.
Ooo, you're my everything, only you know how to free
  all the love there is in me.
I wanna let you know, I won't let you go.
I wanna let you know, I won't let you go.
Ooo, feels so good!

RUN TO YOU

Words and Music by
JUD FRIEDMAN and ALLAN RICH

RIGHT TIME OF THE NIGHT

Words and Music by
PETER McCANN

Right Time of the Night - 3 - 1

SAVING ALL MY LOVE FOR YOU

Words by GERRY GOFFIN
Music by MICHAEL MASSER

SET THE NIGHT TO MUSIC

Words and Music by
DIANE WARREN

The mo - ment is ours to take,

Set the Night to Music - 6 - 6

SHE BELIEVES IN ME

Words and Music by
STEVE GIBB

Lyrics:

I told her some-day___ if she was my girl___ I could change the world___ with my

lit-tle songs,___ I was wrong. But she has faith___ in me,___

And so I go on try-ing faith-ful-ly,___ And who knows, may-be___ on some

spe-cial night___ If my song is right I will find___ a way,___

SHE'S ALL I EVER HAD

Words and Music by
ROBI ROSA, GEORGE NORIEGA
and JON SECADA

Moderately slow ♩ = 82

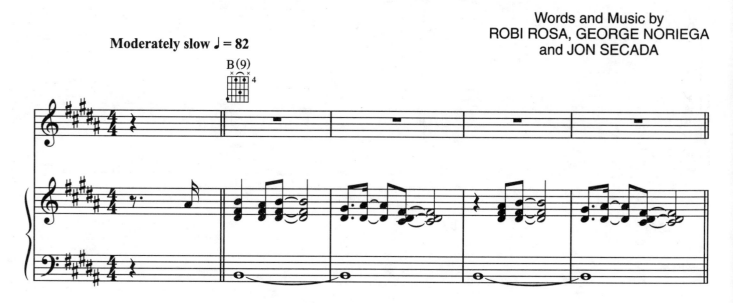

Verse:

1. Here I am,___ bro - ken wings.___
2. So much time,___ so much pain, but

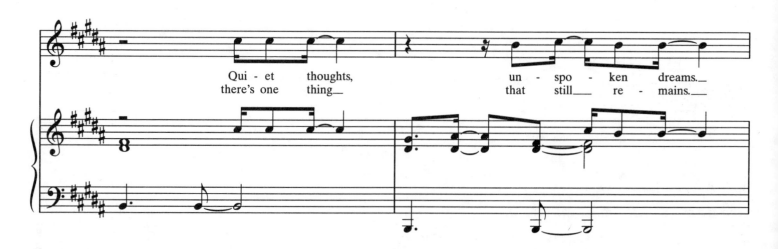

Qui - et thoughts, un - spo - ken dreams.___
there's one thing___ that still___ re - mains.___

She's All I Ever Had - 6 - 1

Lyrics under the music:

And when I look in-to___ her eyes,__ it's the way I feel__ in-side,__

like the man I want_ to be.___ She's all___ I'll ev-er need.__

Chord symbols: B, F#/B, E, *To Coda* ⊕ Em6, B(9)

1. 2.

SLOW HAND

Words and Music by
MICHAEL CLARK and JOHN BETTIS

Slow Hand - 4 - 1

SMOKE GETS IN YOUR EYES

Lyrics by
OTTO HARBACH

Music by
JEROME KERN

STRANGERS IN THE NIGHT

Words by
CHARLES SINGLETON
and EDDIE SNYDER

Music by
BERT KAEMPFERT

* *Chord names and diagrams for guitar.*

Strangers in the Night - 3 - 1

SOMETHING ABOUT THE WAY
YOU LOOK TONIGHT

Lyrics by
BERNIE TAUPIN

Music by
ELTON JOHN

There was a time____ I was ev-ery-thing and no-thing all in one.____

When you found me____ I was feel-ing like a cloud a-cross the sun.____

Something About the Way You Look Tonight - 4 - 1

SUDDENLY

By
KEITH DIAMOND and
BILLY OCEAN

Suddenly - 3 - 1

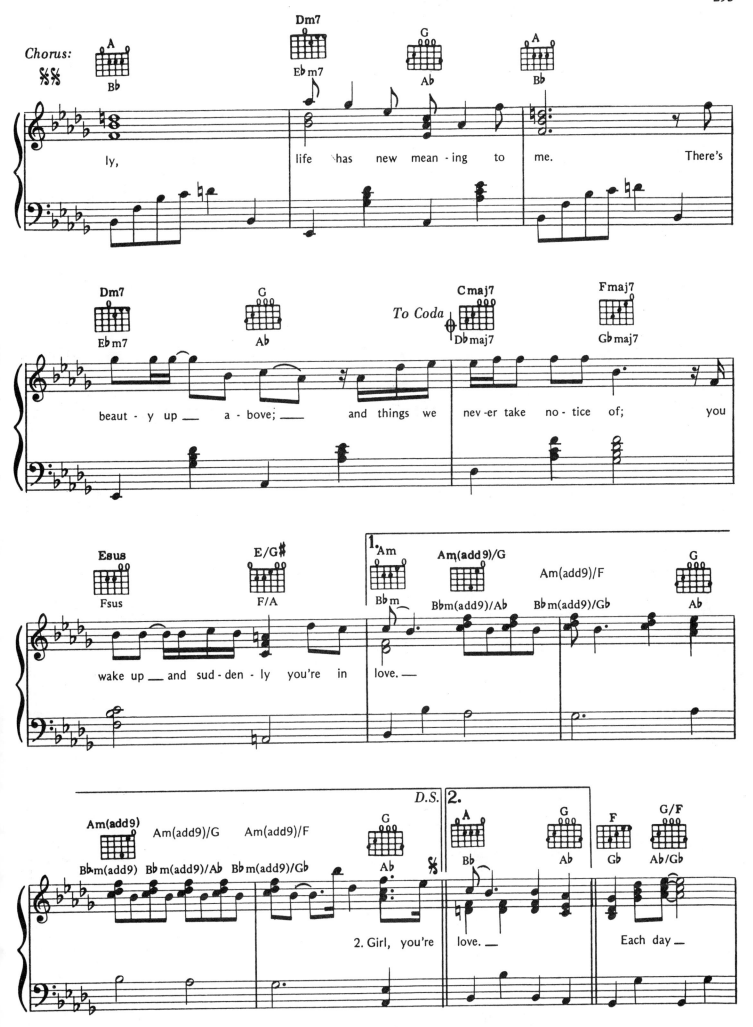

Verse 2:
Girl, you're everything a man could want and more,
One thousand words are not enough
To say what I feel inside,
Holding hands as we walk along the shore
Never felt like this before,
Now you're all I'm living for.

From Touchstone Pictures' PEARL HARBOR

THERE YOU'LL BE

Words and Music by
DIANE WARREN

Chorus:

Chorus:

TELL HIM

Words and Music by
LINDA THOMPSON, DAVID FOSTER
and WALTER AFANASIEFF

Verse 2:
(Barbra:)
Touch him with the gentleness you feel inside. (C: I feel it.)
Your love can't be denied.
The truth will set you free.
You'll have what's meant to be.
All in time, you'll see.
(Celine:)
I love him, (B: Then show him.)
Of that much I can be sure. (B: Hold him close to you.)
I don't think I could endure
If I let him walk away
When I have so much to say.
(To Chorus:)

THEN CAME YOU

Words and Music by
PHIL PUGH and SHERMAN MARSHALL

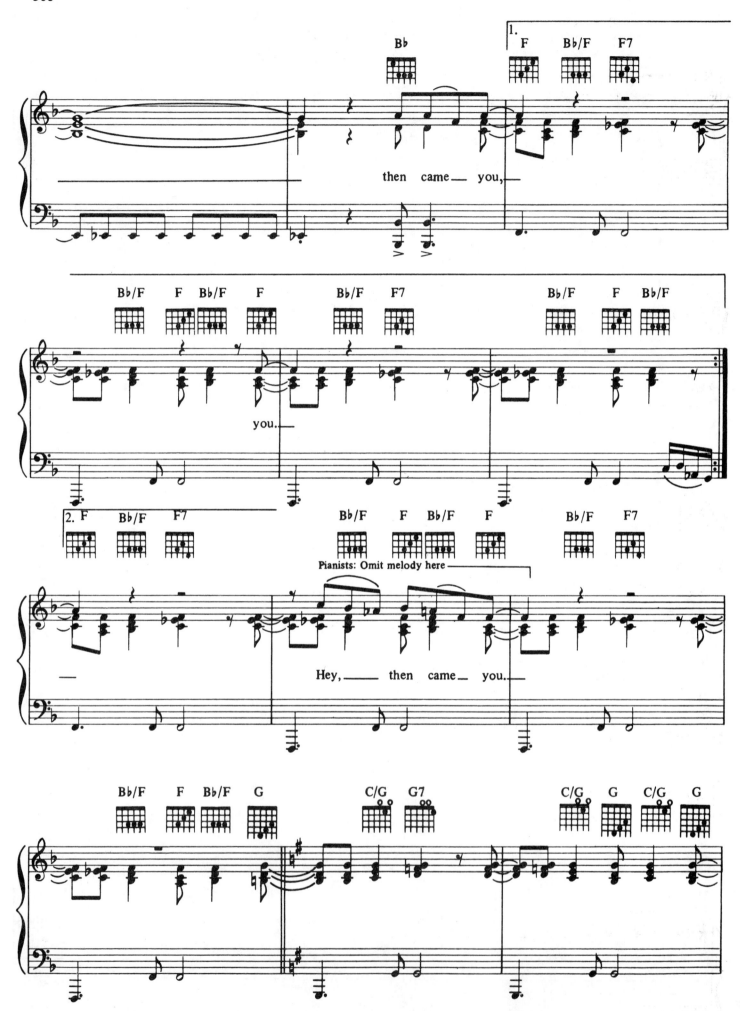

Then Came You - 4 - 4

TO LOVE YOU MORE

Words and Music by
JUNIOR MILES and DAVID FOSTER

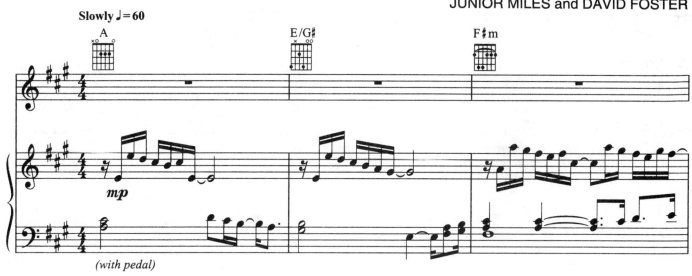

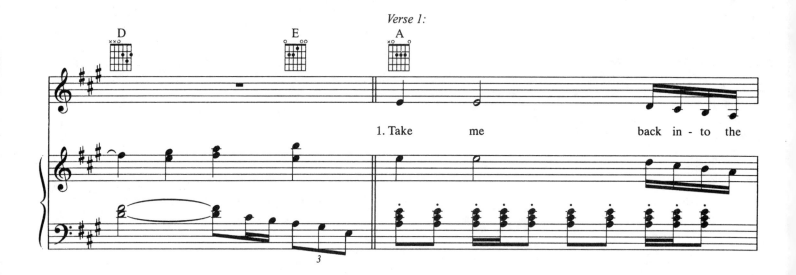

To Love You More - 7 - 1

TRULY

Words and Music by
LIONEL RICHIE

318

TOO LATE TO TURN BACK NOW

Words and Music by
EDDIE CORNELIUS

My ma-ma told___ me, she said, "Son, please be-ware,___

There's this thing called love,___ and it's ah ev-'ry-where."___ And she told me

it can break your heart,___ And put you in___ mis-er-y,___

Too Late to Turn Back Now - 4 - 1

WHEN A MAN LOVES A WOMAN

Words and Music by
CALVIN LEWIS and ANDREW WRIGHT

When a man____ loves a wom-an, can't keep his mind on noth-in' else.
man____ loves a wom-an, spend his ver-y last dime

He'd trade the world for a good thing he's found. If she is bad,____ he can't
try-ing to hold on to what he needs. He'd give up all____ his

When a Man Loves a Woman - 4 - 1

WHEN I SAID I DO

Words and Music by
CLINT BLACK

Verse 2:
Well, this old world keeps changin'
And the world stays the same
For all who came before.
And it goes hand in hand,
Only you and I can undo
All that we became.
That makes us so much more

Than a woman and a man.
And after everything that comes and goes around
Has only passed us by,
Here alone in our dreams,
I know there's a lonely heart in every lost and found.
But forever you and I will be the ones
Who found out what forever means.
(To Chorus:)

2 BECOME 1

Words and Music by
**SPICE GIRLS, MATTHEW ROWEBOTTOM
and RICHARD STANNARD**

Verse 2:

Silly games that you were playing, empty words we both were saying,
Let's work it out boy, let's work it out boy.
Any deal that we endeavour, boys and girls feel good together,
Take it or leave it, take it or leave it.
Are you as good as I remember baby, get it on, get it on,
'Cause tonight is the night when two become one.

I need some love like I never needed love before, (wanna make love to ya baby.)
I had a little love, now I'm back for more, (wanna make love to ya baby.)
Set your spirit free, it's the only way to be.

WHEN I NEED YOU

Words by
CAROLE BAYER SAGER

Music by
ALBERT HAMMOND

When I need you, I just close my eyes and I'm with you and

When I Need You - 5 - 1

When I Need You - 5 - 3

WORDS GET IN THE WAY

Words and Music by
GLORIA ESTEFAN

Words Get In the Way - 3 - 1

Verse 2:
But I know when you have something on your mind.
You've been trying to tell me for the longest time.
And before you break my heart in two,
There's something I've been trying to say to you.

(To Chorus:)

Verse 3:
Your heart has always been an open door,
But baby, I don't even know you any more.
And despite the fact it's hurting me,
I know the time has come to set you free.

(To Chorus:)

YOU'RE STILL THE ONE

Words and Music by
SHANIA TWAIN and R.J. LANGE

You're Still the One - 3 - 1

346

You're Still the One - 3 - 2

Verse 2:
Ain't nothin' better,
We beat the odds together.
I'm glad we didn't listen.
Look at what we would be missin'
(To Bridge:)

LADY

Words and Music by
LIONEL RICHIE

Moderately slow, with feeling

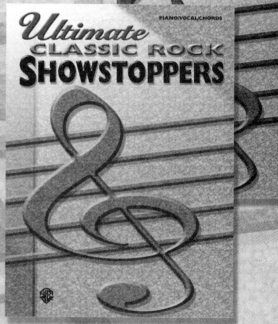
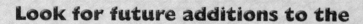